ON THE JOB
Creative Careers

Be a GRAPHIC DESIGNER!

Theresa Emminizer

PowerKiDS press

Published in 2025 by The Rosen Publishing Group, Inc.
2544 Clinton Street, Buffalo, NY 14224

Copyright © 2025 by The Rosen Publishing Group, Inc.

All rights reserved. No part of this book may be reproduced in any form without permission in writing from the publisher, except by a reviewer.

First Edition

Editor: Theresa Emminizer
Book Design: Michael Flynn

Photo Credits: Cover, p. 11 wavebreakmedia/Shutterstock.com; (series background) KanokpolTokumhnerd/Shutterstock.com; (series boxes) vector illustration/Shutterstock.com; p. 5 Rawpixel.com/Shutterstock.com; p. 7 PQK/Shutterstock.com; p. 9 wichayada suwanachun/Shutterstock.com; p. 13 Angelina Dimitrova/Shutterstock.com; p. 15 https://en.wikipedia.org/wiki/File:Eye-Bee-M-Poster.jpg; p. 17 Kaspars Grinvalds/Shutterstock.com; p. 19 Owlie Productions/Shutterstock.com; p. 21 Monkey Business Images/Shutterstock.com; pp. 23, 26 Pixel-Shot/Shutterstock.com; p. 25 Pratchaya.Lee/Shutterstock.com; p. 27 dean bertoncelj/Shutterstock.com; p. 29 Ground Picture/Shutterstock.com.

Cataloging-in-Publication Data

Names: Emminizer, Theresa.
Title: Be a graphic designer! / Theresa Emminizer.
Description: Buffalo, NY : PowerKids Press, 2025. | Series: On the job: creative careers | Includes glossary and index.
Identifiers: ISBN 9781499449488 (pbk.) | ISBN 9781499449495 (library bound) | ISBN 9781499449501 (ebook)
Subjects: LCSH: Graphic arts–Vocational guidance–Juvenile literature. | Graphic artists–Juvenile literature. | Web site development–Vocational guidance–Juvenile literature.
Classification: LCC NC1001.E49 2025 | DDC 741.6203–dc23

Manufactured in the United States of America

Some of the images in this book illustrate individuals who are models. The depictions do not imply actual situations or events.

CPSIA Compliance Information: Batch #CWPK25. For Further Information contact Rosen Publishing at 1-800-237-9932.

CONTENTS

What's Graphic Design? 4

Careers in Graphic Design 6

Elements of Design. 10

Education. 14

Creating a Portfolio 16

Special Skills. 18

Work Environments 20

Schedule and Lifestyle 22

Salary. 24

A World of Design 26

Is Graphic Design for You? 28

Glossary 30

For More Information. 31

Index 32

WHAT'S GRAPHIC DESIGN?

Do you have an eye for art? Do you notice colors and forms? Do you love to draw, paint, and create? If so, then graphic design might be the career path for you!

Graphic design is the art of using visuals, or pictures, to communicate ideas. Graphic designers work in many different fields including **marketing** and publishing. Good graphic design work is eye-catching and memorable, or easy-to-remember.

Graphic designers use different forms of media, or artistic tools, to create their work. But a graphic designer's most powerful tool is their own imagination!

Graphic designers use computers to create and edit images and designs.

CAREERS IN GRAPHIC DESIGN

Graphic designers make all sorts of different products. They may edit pictures, design websites and apps, create designs for apparel, or clothing, and more! Each kind of graphic design job has its own set of responsibilities, or duties, and skills.

A user interface (UI) designer makes sure that a website or app is easy for someone to use. Having basic computer coding and programming skills helps UI designers.

An advertising designer creates billboards, magazine ads, and other kinds of marketing materials. These kinds of designers need a strong background in marketing and a knowledge of what kind of customers, or buyers, they're selling to.

LEARNING ON THE JOB!

Creating one-of-a-kind logos is an important graphic design job. A logo is a company's symbol, or mark. Having a memorable logo helps a company or product stand out.

Graphic designer Milton Glaser (1929–2020) created the famous "I ♡ NY" logo.

Multimedia designers create moving images. They may work on films, television, or video games. They sketch, or draw, make models, and use computer graphics to bring their ideas to life.

Publication designers create designs and layouts for books, magazines, newspapers, and online publications. Some of the most impactful designs, or designs of lasting importance, have been book covers and movie posters.

Art directors work in every field of graphic design. Their job is to oversee all design projects to make sure they fit with a group's vision, or idea of how they want to be seen.

LEARNING ON THE JOB!

Alan Fletcher (1931–2006) was a key figure who helped shape the world of graphic design. Fletcher created **iconic** imagery for Penguin Books. He also helped found Pentagram, an important design firm.

Graphic designers often use special computer tablets called drawing tablets, graphics tablets, or art tablets.

ELEMENTS OF DESIGN

No matter what kind of product they are designing, there are certain design elements that all graphic designers need to keep in mind:

typography: Typography is all about letters, what they look like, and how they're arranged. Fonts are different styles of type.

colors: Different colors evoke, or bring to mind, different feelings. Colors can be playful or serious. They can draw your eye or create depth in an image.

shapes: Certain shapes communicate certain ideas. Lines can draw a person's eye and connect one thing to another. Curves and waves can create movement in an image.

LEARNING ON THE JOB!

Paula Scher is a famous graphic designer who uses typography in a distinctive, or special, way. Her designs often use type as part of an image, instead of a separate element.

A color wheel is a tool that designers use. It shows how different colors work together.

Other design elements include textures, imagery, and space. Texture is the way something feels when you touch it. Even if an image is two-dimensional, or flat, a designer can still show texture. Imagery can include pictures, photos, and illustrations, or drawings.

Space refers to the part of the design that isn't filled up with images, type, or other elements. Although it's easy to overlook, space is a key part of an eye-catching design. Having a lot of space can make a single image pop. Having little space can convey, or communicate, a feeling of excitement or busyness.

LEARNING ON THE JOB!

The art of design is about evoking emotions. White space gives a feeling of cleanliness and calm. White space is especially important in UI design.

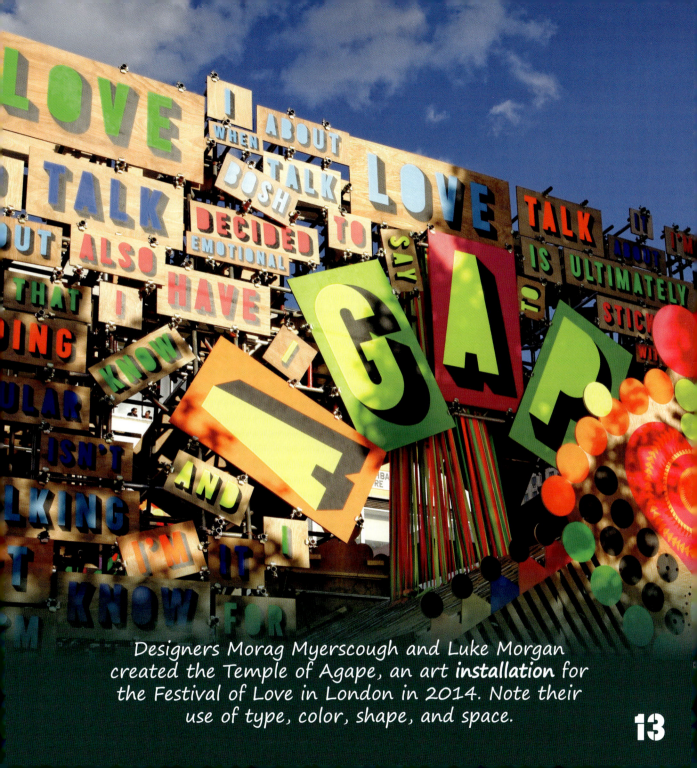

Designers Morag Myerscough and Luke Morgan created the Temple of Agape, an art **installation** for the Festival of Love in London in 2014. Note their use of type, color, shape, and space.

EDUCATION

What kind of education does a graphic designer need? It's recommended, or suggested, that graphic designers have at least an associate's (two year) degree from a college or university. A bachelor's (four year) degree is preferred.

In college, students learn the basics of visual principles, color, typography, web design, and multimedia design. Some graphic designers choose to **pursue** a master's degree in a specialized field. A master's degree is an additional two years beyond a bachelor's degree.

Most employers will look for a candidate, or worker being considered for a job, with a degree in graphic design, fine arts, or visual communication.

LEARNING ON THE JOB!

Pratt Institute, Savannah College of Art and Design, Yale University, and Rhode Island School of Design are some of the top schools for graphic design in the United States.

Paul Rand (1914– 1996) created this iconic logo for IBM. Rand was educated at Pratt Institute.

CREATING A PORTFOLIO

Graphic designers need to build a portfolio to show to schools and employers. A portfolio is a collection of a graphic designer's best work and projects. More than that, it's a way for a designer to show people who they are!

A good portfolio should show a designer's range of abilities, or skills. It should show how they can manipulate, or skillfully use, the different elements of design to communicate a message. A portfolio should also highlight strengths without being too crowded with designs. It could be organized by themes or in order of when the designs were made to show how the designer has grown over time.

It's a good idea to include recommendations, or praise, from past employers or **clients** in a portfolio.

SPECIAL SKILLS

Graphic designers need many **technical** skills including typography, photo editing, and a deep understanding of design principles. They also need several other special skills to be successful.

Graphic designers often need to meet tough deadlines. To do this, they need to be able to manage their time well. They also often need to work within a budget, or certain amount of money for a project.

Graphic designers also need to be able to collaborate, or work together, with others to reach a common goal. They need to communicate clearly. Most importantly, they must be creative! Graphic designers think outside the box and use their imaginations.

Graphic designers often work in teams.

WORK ENVIRONMENTS

Where do graphic designers work? Many work in design studios, or work spaces for artists. Some work in offices. Others work at home!

No matter their surroundings, most graphic designers spend a lot of time on computers. They need a strong ability to focus, or pay attention, without being able to move around a lot. Graphic design work often involves reworking the same project over and over again. After their work is reviewed by coworkers, directors, or clients, designers may need to make changes based on feedback from others. This can be a long, tricky process that requires patience and problem-solving abilities.

Graphic designers need good equipment, or tools, to do their work well.

SCHEDULE AND LIFESTYLE

A designer's **schedule** depends on what kind of job they have. Freelance designers have a project-based schedule. They may spend many hours a week working on a single project until it's completed, but they may have little to do until they're contracted, or hired by an agreement, to do more work.

A designer who works at a design agency, or business, usually works a full-time schedule. That means they work eight hours a day and 40 hours a week. However, when meeting deadlines or tackling many projects, full-time workers may work up to 60 hours a week.

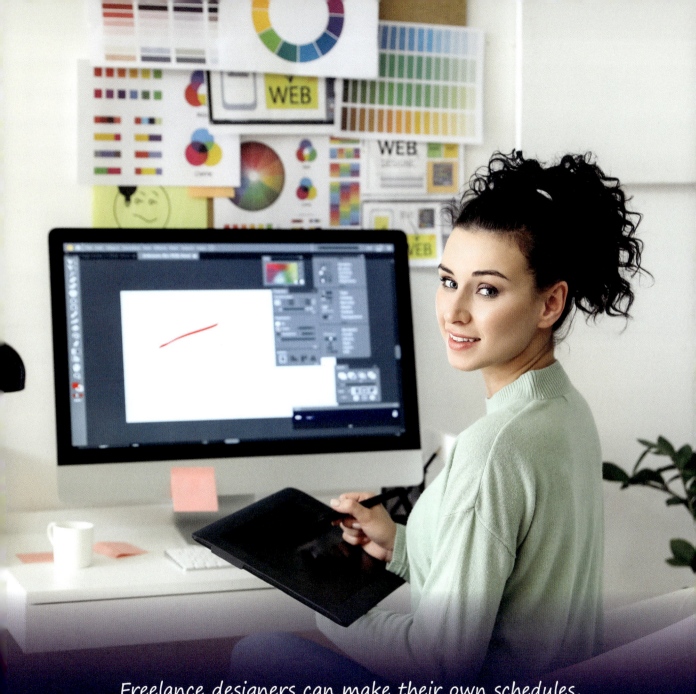
Freelance designers can make their own schedules, but don't have the stability of a full-time job.

SALARY

How much money can a graphic designer expect to make? A designer's salary depends on a few different factors: the design field, their level of education and experience, and their expertise, or special knowledge.

The average salary for a graphic designer in the United States is about $64,700 a year. Entry level, or beginner, design jobs pay about $55,951 a year on average. An art director may make around $106,500 a year.

The top paying companies for graphic designers are Microsoft, Dropbox, X, Apple, and Google. Some designers may make upward of $150,000 a year at these companies.

Median annual wages, May 2023

Graphic designers — $58,910

Art and design workers — $51,660

Total, all occupations — $48,060

As of 2022, about 51.9 percent of graphic designers in the United States were female.

A WORLD OF DESIGN

Graphic designers are some of the greatest artists of our time. Their **influence** surrounds us. Their work lasts long beyond their lifetime.

One of the things that makes graphic design so exciting is that it allows you to **express** yourself and leave your mark on the world. Look around you. The work of graphic designers is part of your life every day! Pick up a book and notice the cover design. Check out a billboard as you drive down the street. Look more closely at the layout of your favorite website or app. Graphic design is all around you!

Some of the most iconic graphic design work has been made for music album covers.

IS GRAPHIC DESIGN FOR YOU?

Does graphic design sound like the right path for you? You don't have to be a grown-up to get started! The best way to grow your skills as a designer is to simply have fun!

Try making a mood board. Cut pictures from magazines and place images and colors next to each other. See how you can place things differently to convey different feelings or ideas. Grab free paint color swatches, or paper samples, from a home goods store and play around with them. Take photos and draw pictures. Practice paying attention to composition, or how elements are arranged in a photo or drawing. Look, feel, and create!

Do you have an eye for design?

GLOSSARY

client: Someone who pays a professional for a certain service.

express: To communicate what you're thinking or feeling.

iconic: A symbol that is widely known.

influence: An effect one thing has on another.

installation: A work of art with multiple parts that is often shown in a large space.

marketing: Working to spread awareness about a company's products and making sure people can buy those products.

pursue: To go after something.

schedule: A plan of things to get done with times for accomplishing them.

technical: Having special and usually practical knowledge, especially of a mechanical or scientific subject.

FOR MORE INFORMATION

BOOKS

Müller, Jens. *The History of Graphic Design: 1890– Today*. Cologne: Taschen, 2023.

Van Oosbree, Ruthie. *Designing with Graphic Arts: DIY Visual Projects*. MN: Abdo & Daughters, an imprint of Abdo Publishing, 2023.

WEBSITES

i Camp
icamp.com/graphic-design-for-kids/
Learn more about the elements of design and what kind of design programs you can try out.

The Marginalian
www.themarginalian.org/2013/10/22/chip-kidd-go-book/
Read famous designer Chip Kidd's introduction to the world of graphic design.

Publisher's note to educators and parents: Our editors have carefully reviewed these websites to ensure that they are suitable for students. Many websites change frequently, however, and we cannot guarantee that a site's future contents will continue to meet our high standards of quality and educational value. Be advised that students should be closely supervised whenever they access the internet.

INDEX

A
advertising designer, 6
art directors, 8, 24

B
budget, 18

C
color, 4, 10, 11, 13, 14, 28
composition, 28
computers, 5, 6, 8, 9, 20

D
deadlines, 18, 22
degrees, 14
design agency, 22

E
employers, 14, 16, 17

F
feedback, 20
Fletcher, Alan, 8
focus, 20
freelance designers, 22, 23

L
logos, 7, 15

M
money, 18, 24
mood board, 28
multimedia designers, 8

P
publication designers, 8

S
schools, 15, 16
shapes, 10, 13
space, 12, 13

T
Temple of Agape, 13
textures, 12
typography, 10, 14, 18

U
user interface (UI) design, 6, 12